My Little Book of Thank You Prayers

Written and compiled by
Felicity Henderson

Illustrations by
Toni Goffe

A LION BOOK

Tring . Batavia . Sydney

Thank you

Thank you for the world so sweet,
Thank you for the food we eat.
Thank you for the birds that sing,
Thank you, God, for everything.

God is great

God is great, God is good,
Thank you, God, for all our food.

Moms and dads

Thank you, God,
for our moms and dads who love us
and take care of us.

Grandmas and grandpas

Thank you, Lord,
for grandmas and grandpas.
Thank you for the stories they tell us
and the things they help us make.
Thank you that they have the time
to tie up our shoes and take us for walks.
Please bless them all.

Pets

O Lord God,
Thank you for making
all the animals.
And thank you for
our pets — for rabbits
and guinea-pigs,
cats and dogs.

My friend

At my friend's house today
we played dressing up.
And then we had supper.
Thank you for my friend.

Sisters and brothers

My big sister looks after me.
Sometimes she reads me stories.
My baby brother is always hungry,

but when he smiles, he's lovely.
Thank you, God,
for my brother and sister.

The world God has made

Trees and flowers,
Sky and sea,
God made everything.
And God made me!

God loves me!

Mom says you think I'm special,
And that you love me lots!
Thank you, God.

New clothes

Today Mom went shopping.
I got a new track-suit.
Thank you, God, for my new clothes.

God's family

We thank you, God, that everyone
who loves you belongs to your family.
You are our Father, we are your children.
Thank you, God, for the worldwide
family of your people.
Thank you for our brothers
and sisters the whole world over.

The rainbow

Dear God, thank you
for all the lovely colors
of the rainbow.

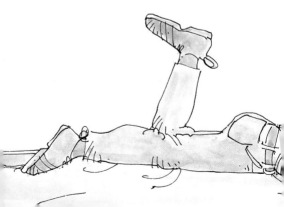

God's love

All good gifts around us
Are sent from heaven above;
Then thank the Lord, O thank the Lord,
For all his love.

Text copyright © 1988 Lion Publishing
Illustrations copyright © 1988 Toni Goffe

Published by
Lion Publishing plc
Icknield Way, Tring, Herts, England
ISBN 0 7459 1254 0
Lion Publishing Corporation
1705 Hubbard Avenue, Batavia, Illinois 60510, USA
ISBN 0 7459 1254 0
Albatross Books Pty Ltd
PO Box 320, Sutherland, NSW 2232, Australia
ISBN 0 86760 941 9

First edition 1988

Acknowledgments
Copyright prayers as follows:
'Thank you for the world so sweet' from
Hymns and Songs for Children, National Society;
'God is great, God is good' from *Little Folded Hands,*
Concordia Publishing House Ltd;
'Thank you, Lord, for grannies and grandads'
by Mary Batchelor from *The Lion Book of
Children's Prayers,* Lion Publishing.

Printed and bound in Singapore